W9-CUW-751

PET OWNER'S GUIDE TO THE
BEARDED DRAGON

Aidan Raftery
MVB CertZooMed MRCVS

RINGPRESS

ABOUT THE AUTHOR

Aidan Raftery MVB CertZooMed MRCVS is a specialist in exotic animals. He is board-certified in Zoological Medicine and Surgery by the Royal College of Veterinary Surgeons.

He now works in the Avian and Exotic Animal Clinic in Chorlton, Manchester, where he sees mainly referrals from other veterinarians, and clinical cases from several licensed zoos. He also lectures both within the UK and overseas.

Aidan has kept and bred many different species of reptiles. Bearded Dragons are his particular favourites and he currently maintains a happy community of three Bearded Dragons who successfully breed every year.

PHOTOGRAPHY
Fred Holmes

Published by Ringpress Books,
A Division of INTERPET LTD,
Vincent Lane, Dorking, Surrey, RH4 3YX

First published 2002
This reprint 2008
©2002 Ringpress Books. All rights reserved

Design: Rob Benson

ISBN 978 1 86054 129 2

Printed in China through Printworks Int. Ltd.

CONTENTS

1

INTRODUCING THE BEARDED DRAGON 6

Origin; Appearance; Habitat; Diet; Inland Bearded Dragons; Pogona types; Responsibility.

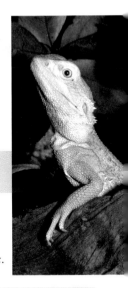

2

CHOOSING A BEARDED DRAGON 12

Where to buy; What to look for; Assessment (Good qualities; Bad points); The right age (Size chart); How many? What sex?; Interpreting display; Colour code; Going home.

3

SETTING UP HOME 22

Space; Vivaria (Position; Temperature); Heat sources (Basking lights; Additional heat; Night-time); Water; Substrates; Decor; Photo-periods; Thermostats (Thermometers); UV light (UV/vitamin D3; Environmental control systems; Sunlight; Full-spectrum); Outdoor enclosures (Protection; Humidity; Temperature; Soil care); Brumation.

4

ROUTINE CARE 38

Handling (Support; Tails; Harnesses); Nails (Natural wear; Trimming; Bleeding); House-training; Exercising; Cleaning (Cleaning kit; Disinfectants; Isolation); Routines (Daily; Monthly; Half-yearly); Salmonella alert (Hygiene; At risk).

5

DIET AND FEEDING 47

Plants; Live food (Preparation; Dangers);
Formulated diets; Mice; Adults
(Insects/mice; Water); Juveniles (Insects;
Water); Hatchlings (Insects; Water); Fussy
Eaters; Supplements (Balance).

6

BREEDING AND REARING 57

Sexual maturity; Nests; Preparation (Environment; The
animals); Breeding; Laying (Supplements); Nesting; Maternity;
Incubators (Position; Substrate); Incubation; Hatchlings
(Housing; Temperature; Diet; Rehoming).

7

HEALTH CARE 67

Veterinarians; Internet info; Common ailments (Dental
Disease; Mouth rot; Shedding); Parasites (Internal; External);
Tremors; Breathing; Egg-binding; Diarrhoea; Dehydration;
Wounds; Burns; Fractures; Hyperthermia.

1 Introducing The Bearded Dragon

Bearded Dragons are lizards of a moderate size, that have a good temperament and are easy to tame. They are very sociable and interact with one another, using a complex set of body gestures, including head bobs, arm circling movements, body tilts and differing tail and head postures, together with other more subtle movements.

They also socialise and interact with humans who are familiar to them. Fully-grown adults vary in length from 45 to 60 centimetres (18 to 24 inches) and are relatively easy to breed. As a result of these attributes, their popularity as pets is rapidly increasing.

ORIGIN
The continent of Australia

The Bearded Dragon is one of the most popular of the exotic pets to keep.

The black beard is flared out as a form of sexual display, or when the Bearded Dragon feels threatened.

separated from South America and Antarctica about 55 million years ago and has subsequently existed in splendid isolation from the rest of the earth's land masses.

As a consequence, animal life in Australia evolved untouched by outside influences for many centuries and possesses unique attributes, from egg-laying mammals with beaks to stomach-brooding frogs, from mammals that hop and carry their young in pouches to frilled lizards.

Australia has an amazing variety of snakes and lizards, which fill the many and varied ecological niches available on that enormous continent. Bearded Dragons are among the unique fauna that evolved there in isolation. They are found only in Eastern and Central Australia.

Bearded Dragons are not regarded as a threatened species in Australia. Even in areas where the habitat is degraded, their numbers appear to be stable, unlike many other native Australian animals.

In areas where comparatively recently introduced predators, such as foxes and cats, have displaced many of the native animals, the population density of Bearded Dragons is only reduced where there is a high concentration of cats.

APPEARANCE

Bearded Dragons get their name from their distinctive throat, which can be flared out to make them look bigger, either when they are threatened or, in males, when they are displaying to sexually mature females. The

The body is covered with scales.

colour of that 'beard' will, at the same time, turn black.

In addition to displaying the black beard, they also flatten their body to make themselves look wider, and then they enhance the effect with a gaping mouth. These displays are most impressive in dominant males.

Captive Bearded Dragons rarely feel the need to put on such a show. However, in large enclosures, where two males and several females are housed together, the males will be seen to display, especially when they are establishing a pecking order.

Bearded Dragons have broad, triangular-shaped heads, a flat body and a relatively short tail. The body is covered with scales which, on the throat and the sides of the head, have specialised spiny points. The scales covering the rest

of the body also have these spiny points but they are carried flatter to the body.

Coloration is usually a brownish-red background, with the pattern on the head and body a yellow gold. The underside of the body is a much paler colour.

Breeders take advantage of the normal degree of colour variation between individuals (even from the same clutch of eggs), between different regional populations and from the occasional mutation, to breed selectively for different colours. The results are known as 'colour morphs' which can be equated to breeds of domesticated animals.

HABITAT

In the areas of Australia where Bearded Dragons live, the climate varies from arid to semi-arid and the vegetation ranges from rocky outcrops to open woodland. These lizards are not found in dense woodland. The hottest parts of the day are spent in the relative cool of burrows or under boulders. In the mornings and afternoons, they will often be found basking on rocks, on branches, or on fence posts in farmland areas, in order to raise their body temperature in preparation for foraging for food.

INTRODUCING THE BEARDED DRAGON

In times of extended adverse conditions, when it is either very hot or too cold, Bearded Dragons will go into a dormant state for long periods. This time is spent in burrows or under boulders, or sometimes they dig into the ground.

DIET

Bearded Dragons eat a wide variety of plant and animal material in the wild. They are true omnivores – which means they will eat anything that takes their fancy.

They will not eat tough vegetative material like branches or twigs, nor will they eat highly fibrous plant material such as grasses. They eat mainly green leafy plant material and, when available in their environment, flowers and fruit.

Most types of insects are eaten voraciously. Given the opportunity, Bearded Dragons will also take small mammals. This happens less often in Australia, as all the small mammals are marsupial and the young are carried around by the mothers in pouches until they are further advanced.

There is a smaller window of opportunity when relatively vulnerable marsupial young are

In the wild, Bearded Dragons are found basking on rocks or on branches.

Rankin's Dragon: This species is becoming more widely available.

unprotected by the mother and can be taken as food by predators the size of Bearded Dragons.

INLAND BEARDED DRAGONS

Pogona vitticeps, the inland Bearded Dragon, is the species referred to in the pet trade as the Bearded Dragon. Other species of Bearded Dragon are maintained in captivity in much smaller numbers and are rarely offered for sale. This book is about *Pogona vitticeps,* but all the housing, diet and environmental information will equally apply, with minor modifications, to other species of Bearded Dragon.

Australia's very strict conservation laws now prohibit the export of reptiles, with the result that all Australian reptiles available to herpetologists outside Australia will be captive-bred. All Bearded Dragons in the pet trade appear to have originated from founder animals first imported into Germany.

POGONA TYPES

Bearded Dragons are agamid lizards. This means that they are classified in a family of lizards called the *Agamidae* which have anatomical similarities. Included in this family are Water Dragons, Spiny-tailed Agamids, Thorny Devils, Frilled Lizards and the Butterfly Lizard.

Within that group, Bearded Dragons belong to the genus *Pogona*, formerly *Amphibolurus*. Older books will list them as *Amphibolurus vitticeps*. There are seven species in the genus *Pogona*.

- *Pogona vitticeps*: the inland Bearded Dragon. This species is most commonly kept as pets, and is the subject of this book.
- *Pogona barbata*: the common Bearded Dragon. Very small numbers are present in captivity. They do not have the same personality as the inland Bearded Dragon and are more difficult to breed and rear.
- *Pogona henrylawsoni*: Rankin's Dragon (sometimes also called Lawson's Dragon or the black-soil Bearded Dragon). This species is becoming more widely available but is still very rare compared with the inland Bearded Dragon. It should not really qualify as a Bearded Dragon as it does not display a beard. Like the Inland Bearded Dragon, they quickly get to know their owners and become very tame.
- *Pogona minima:* The Western Bearded Dragon. This species, and the following three, are not currently available to herpetoculture due to Australia's very strict conservation laws.
- *Pogona minor:* The Dwarf Bearded Dragon.
- *Pogona mitchelli:* The North-west Bearded Dragon.
- *Pogona nullarbor:* The Nullarbor Bearded Dragon.

RESPONSIBILITY

Bearded Dragons are relatively long-lived lizards. With good husbandry they will, on average, live to between seven and ten years of age.

Currently, many Bearded Dragons are not surviving beyond four or five years of age, however. This is mainly due to a legacy of having been fed the wrong diet in the first years of life.

However, as the correct information on how to keep and feed Bearded Dragons becomes more widely disseminated, they are beginning to live healthier lives for longer in captivity.

2 Choosing A Bearded Dragon

If you really want to embark on the responsible hobby of reptile-keeping and wish to start with a Bearded Dragon, then look around, talk to people, learn as much as possible and go to a reputable pet store which is knowledgeable about lizards, snakes and geckos.

Do bear in mind, before you buy any animals, that you must have the appropriate accommodation ready and waiting for them when you bring them to your home.

WHERE TO BUY
Read this book before you buy a vivarium, its furniture, or a Bearded Dragon, so that you will have a basic understanding of the animal's needs and will be able to assess the level of knowledge possessed by the people selling it. Be sure to speak to the 'Bearded Dragon expert' in the pet store. If you find the level of knowledge is low and you are being given incorrect information, then buy from another store.

In pet stores where there is just an illusion of knowledge, the animals will not have been cared for correctly and may, depending on how long they have been in the shop, already be suffering from nutritional and environmentally-related diseases.

A pet store with knowledgeable staff will also be more likely to stock the equipment needed to set up the vivarium correctly.

WHAT TO LOOK FOR
The aim of this chapter is to help you to recognise a healthy Bearded Dragon. In general, use common sense and do not choose an animal that does not look healthy or is withdrawn.

Bearded Dragons are lively, inquisitive, active lizards. They should be alert and interested in their environment.

Look for bright eyes, and an alert, upright posture.

GOOD QUALITIES

Check out the following signs:

- The lizard should have an alert attitude.
- The eyes should be wide open and active, following any movement.
- The lizard should have an upright posture.
- There should be a wide stance of the fore legs and the front of the body should be raised off the ground, especially when disturbed.
- Look for a well-filled-out belly.
- The outline of the spine and the hip bones should not be visible.
- The skin should feel tight to the body and not loose, which might indicate weight loss.
- The Bearded Dragon should be eating appropriate food and not being picky. Enquire about what it is being offered and what is eaten.
- The lizard should show a willingness to bask.
- There must be an absence of swellings.
- The stools should be solid.
- The mouth should be clean and pink in colour. The gums should also be a healthy pink colour, free from any swellings or crusty build-up.
- If any toes, or a part of the tail is missing, these will not regrow.

BAD POINTS

If you see any of the following, do not go ahead with your purchase.

• *The young Bearded Dragon who has not been accustomed to eating a good diet.*

Always ask what it has been offered and what it has eaten. Is it a picky eater? Such an animal may be difficult to convert to a more nutritionally-correct diet, and this will lead to long-term health problems.

Growing up on a poor diet will not result in a healthy adult. Vitamin and mineral supplements are no substitute for a correct diet, though they may help the animal who is beginning to improve in health. Additionally, animals that are picky eaters may have underlying problems.

• *A lizard that does not bask.* Lizards need to thermo-regulate. This means that they must have the ability to locate a heat source and to bask in its warmth, in order to raise their body temperature to its optimum.

Without achieving this optimum level of heat, they will not have sufficient energy

Try to establish whether there are any feeding problems.

to find food and then to digest it. Those that do not thermo-regulate efficiently are best avoided. They, too, may often have underlying problems.

- *A Bearded Dragon with any swelling visible on the body, limbs, tail or toes.*

  These may indicate a problem that has spread to internal areas, which is not easily detectable, and may reveal itself as a major health problem at a later date.

- *A vivarium showing any signs of watery droppings, and a lizard with dark staining around the vent, which might indicate that it has diarrhoea.*

- *A Bearded Dragon that is infected with trombiculoid mites.* These appear as red or orange patches on the skin which, upon close inspection, will be seen to move. Such lizards are occasionally offered for sale. They should be avoided as they can spread other, more serious, internal infections.

THE RIGHT AGE

It is best not to start with a hatchling as they are much more difficult to care for and feed. They are also more vulnerable to even temporary adverse environmental conditions.

Start with a Dragon which is a minimum of two months old. At this age, they should be 15 centimetres (6 inches) long and are more robust about changes in their lifestyle. With lizards younger than two months old, nutrition is critical and they are much more susceptible to health problems. If you can select a slightly older Dragon, this will be better, but they are rarely available.

Ideally, buy a Bearded Dragon at around two months of age.

SIZE CHART

Bearded Dragon size versus age chart (snout to tail tip)

Age	Size Range
1 month	10 to 15 cm (4 to 6 ins)
3 months	15 to 25 cm (6 to 10 ins)
6 months	18 to 38 cm (7 to 15 ins)
9 months	23 to 40 cm (9 to 16 ins)
1 year	30 to 50 cm (12 to 20 ins)
1 year 6 months	38 to 60 cm (15 to 24 ins)

Do not buy an adult Bearded Dragon, as there is no way of estimating its age and it is more likely to have hidden health problems. It may even be a geriatric Bearded Dragon, which would have problems associated with old age.

HOW MANY?

Bearded Dragons can be kept on their own. However, as their social needs are not fully understood, it is preferable to have a larger enclosure and to keep a minimum of two animals together, preferably in sexual pairs (two males together will fight), or in groups with one male and two or more females.

If you intend to get only one Dragon, it is best to choose a male (remember, however, that sexing at this young age is very difficult) as females have a tendency to suffer problems with their ovaries and uterus.

Also remember that Dragons are a social species that do interact with each other much more than other commonly-kept species of reptile.

WHAT SEX?

When they are immature, Bearded Dragons are very difficult to sex accurately.

The commonest method is to compare the tails. In the males, just past the vent, the tail tapers more gradually than in females, which is due to the presence of the inverted hemipenes. Simply put, these are the dual sexual organs of the male lizard.

Another method, often quoted, is to manually evert the hemipenes using digital pressure. However, I do not recommend that this method is used: it is rarely successful with Bearded Dragons and can severely injure the lizard.

Adult lizards are easier to sex, as

SEXING BEARDED DRAGONS

In the male (right), the tail ▶
tapers more gradually than
the female tail (left).

The preanal and femoral pores
are larger in the male (above)
than the female (right).

You may observe differences in behaviour between the two sexes.

the differences in the tail are more obvious. Another method of sexing is by examining the preanal and femoral pores, which are larger in males. The femoral pores are seen as a chain of small swellings on the underside of the thighs and the preanal pores are its continuation in front of the vent. They are the openings to small skin glands. However, they can also occasionally be well developed in females, so the method is not fail-safe.

Head size, which is wider in males, is another indicator of sex, as is the dark throat (beard), which is bigger in males.

During the breeding season, the larger beards of the males are also darker, especially in the presence of receptive females or subordinate males.

Subordinate males may not display the darker beard and their submissive behaviour may mimic that of a female.

The male vent is also much larger than the female's. Pulling the skin back around the vent exposes the opening, which is usually dramatically wider in males.

INTERPRETING DISPLAY

There are behavioural differences

Young Bearded Dragons will be vulnerable to cold conditions.

between sexually-mature males and females which make identifying the sex easier. Males, especially in the breeding season, will extend and display their beards as a sexual display towards females or as an aggressive display towards other males. Head bobbing, fighting with other males and attempting to copulate are all consistent behaviours in males.

Females do a movement which is called arm waving, where they raise one front leg off the ground and move it in a slow arc. This is performed towards the male during the breeding season or during copulation as a receptive or subordinate display.

Juveniles of both sexes will sometimes arm wave as a social interaction and, occasionally, mature males will arm wave in response to a larger, more dominant male.

COLOUR CODE
A genetic colour variation occurs in the Bearded Dragon. The process of breeding different colours of Bearded Dragon is therefore made easier, as there is a relatively wide variation in the wild colour, especially from different regions.

These differences were exploited, along with several individuals that may have been colour mutations, to produce the range of colours that are available today. The more available colour morphs are:

- Red phase: well-defined pattern with a background orange-red colour.
- Sandfire: reduced pattern and colour gold or orange.
- Giant German: larger morph with a relatively smaller head to body.

There are many variations that are crosses between different morphs, with an endless variety of body coloration, pattern and size.

GOING HOME

A secure box to transport your new Bearded Dragon home will be needed. Often the pet store or breeder will provide something suitable. Depending on the outside temperature, some source of heat may be needed to keep the lizard warm on the journey home. A hot water bottle, or similar, will suffice. This should be wrapped in a towel to ensure that there is no direct contact between the lizard and the heat source, which might otherwise cause burns.

In very cold conditions, an insulated box may be required. Some are commercially available, made out of polystyrene. The younger the Dragon purchased, the more vulnerable it is to variations in the environment.

Adult Bearded Dragons, in areas of the world where the climate is suitable, sometimes commute with their owners to second or weekend homes, controlled only by a harness. Dragons that routinely make these trips appear to enjoy the scenery!

3 *Setting Up Home*

In most parts of the world Bearded Dragons have to be kept in an indoor vivarium, although it is possible, in warmer climates, to keep them in outdoor enclosures, either seasonally or all year round.

Wherever you establish their home, certain rules must be adhered to, and two important life-sustaining principles remembered.

• Bearded Dragons, like all reptiles, are ectotherms, which means that they require external sources to heat their bodies. Therefore, they have to be given the opportunity to thermo-regulate.

• Thermo-regulation means that the lizard moves between areas of different temperatures in

Provide the most spacious accommodation you can afford for your Bearded Dragon.

order to regulate its own internal temperature.

SPACE

Bearded Dragons can be kept singly, in sexual pairs, or in groups containing one male with two or more females. If the enclosure is very large, with multiple hiding and basking places, two males and multiple females may be housed together. Some fighting between the males may occur, even in the biggest enclosures.

The minimum enclosure size for the long-term maintenance of a single adult Bearded Dragon would be 180 cm long by 45 cm wide by 40 cm high (72 x 18 x 16 inches/0.8 metres squared flootage.) Where groups are maintained together, increase the floor area by 0.36 metres squared of floor area for every Bearded Dragon added.

These are minimum enclosure sizes. In general, the larger an area which can be provided for them, the better. Do remember, also, that the more Bearded Dragons you keep, the greater will be the requirement for multiple basking lights, feeding stations and full spectrum lights in order to minimise competition – otherwise the weaker individuals will suffer.

VIVARIA

An indoor enclosure is called a vivarium, which can be bought ready-made or constructed at home. A large aquarium can usually be made into a vivarium, but access would have to be from the top and it will be very heavy to move. It is more convenient to have a door on the front, unless the vivarium is to be positioned on the ground.

Vivaria should be constructed from materials that are non-absorbent and easily cleaned. The commercially available ones made of plastic are lightweight. All the corners are rounded for easy cleaning, there are good ventilation grids, and it is easy to fit the necessary lights and heaters into them.

Home-made vivaria are usually made from glass and melamine-faced wood. These have a limited lifespan and are difficult to clean properly.

POSITION

You must take great care when choosing where to place the vivarium. It should not be in the kitchen, or adjacent to any food preparation area, because of the risk of faecal contamination when handling the Bearded Dragon and, especially, when cleaning the vivarium.

It should not be positioned in direct sunlight, as it will then act like a greenhouse and temperatures may quickly rise to lethal levels above 48 degrees C (116 degrees F). This may even happen in winter on a sunny day.

TEMPERATURE
In the vivarium the daytime temperature should range from 25 to 30 degrees C (77 to 86 degrees F), with a basking site temperature range of between 30 and 35 degrees C (86 to 95 degrees F). At night the temperature should drop to between 20 and 22 degrees C (68 to 71.6 degrees F).

The temperature within the vivarium needs to be carefully monitored, especially during the setting-up period. Thermometers that record the maximum and minimum temperatures should be used.

HEAT SOURCES
BASKING LIGHTS
The basking light can be an incandescent light bulb or a special heating bulb, such as a ceramic heater. The only requirement of a basking light is that it radiates

Remember to measure the temperature that the basking light achieves.

heat. It should be positioned at one end of the enclosure to assist in providing a temperature gradient within the enclosure.

Basking lights must be positioned at a high point in the enclosure. Bearded Dragons are genetically conditioned to respond to a heat source from above and like to climb up towards it. They use this heat to bring their body temperature up to optimum before foraging for food and, after eating, to assist their digestion.

Position the basking light at one end. This will be the hot end. Vary the height of the basking lamp (and/or the heat output) to achieve the required temperature at the basking area, which is 30 to 35 degrees C (86 to 95 degrees F). Next, measure the temperature range from the hot end to the cold end. This needs to range from 30 to 25 degrees C (86 to 77 degrees F).

A dark rock, with a flat area on its top, placed under the basking light, will quickly warm up. When used as a basking site by the Bearded Dragon, it will provide additional ventral heat that may aid in digestion. Alternatively, a large log can be positioned under the basking light.

Remember that the basking light will get very hot to touch and must be surrounded by a guard to prevent the Bearded Dragons from burning themselves. If it is well out of reach, this may not be necessary.

ADDITIONAL HEAT

Usually, additional heat sources are needed to achieve the proper temperature range. The most common method is by using a heat mat under the vivarium. Insulate this from the ground, or the work surface on which the vivarium is placed, to ensure that the heat comes up. Alternatively, or additionally, heat mats can be placed around the side walls of the tank – again insulated to ensure that the heat radiates in.

Remember, the lower the ambient temperature surrounding the vivarium, the more difficult it is to achieve the correct temperatures inside it.

The best room in which to position the vivarium is the warmest and best-insulated one, in order to reduce variability in the ambient temperature.

Avoid hot rocks. They are made of clay cement, or plastic formed around a heating coil. As the electric coil heats up, so does the 'rock'.

Hot rocks are notorious for having surface hot spots that reach temperatures capable of giving severe burns. They are a common cause of burns in reptiles. Some new models on the market claim to have solved this problem.

The lizard is expected to climb on to this rock to maintain its body temperature. However, lizards instinctively thermo-regulate in response to radiated heat from above and may not use a hot rock to thermo-regulate properly if it is the only heat source.

The skill is to provide the correct temperature range within the vivarium.

NIGHT-TIME

Check the night-time temperature when the basking light will be off. The required drop in temperature can be achieved by switching all or some of the heating sources off. Use a maximum and minimum thermometer so that the lowest night-time temperature is recorded. It is usually necessary to leave the heat mat, or mats, on. Do not allow the night-time temperature to fall below 17 degrees C (62.6 degrees F).

At night the Bearded Dragon's home should be dark; only red light bulbs can be left on, and these are only necessary if they are being used as a heat source. Twenty-four hours of bright light will stress the lizard and confuse its body clock which, in the long term, will make it more susceptible to disease.

WATER

Always make sure your Dragon has access to plenty of fresh water. A water dish should be positioned in the hot end of the vivarium and kept full of clean potable water. The container should be shallow enough for the Bearded Dragons to be able to drink from it while maintaining a normal stance.

It also needs to be deep enough so that they can submerge their nares (the opening of their nasal cavities) in it while drinking.

Lizards will often defecate in their water, which means the bowl must be cleaned and filled with fresh water daily.

Most Bearded Dragons also like to soak in their water bowl, so it must be heavy enough to prevent it being tipped over if they attempt to climb in for a bath.

The water temperature should

Bearded Dragons need water to drink, and also to bathe in.

be between 24-28 degrees C (75-82F). The water bowl can be moved to a position where the temperature is within the ideal.

SUBSTRATES

Your choice of substrate is very important. The right one is easy to maintain and provides the opportunity to observe the faeces and urates of your animals.

Regardless of which substrate is used, it should be kept clean and dry. Damp areas will quickly grow mould, which, if ingested regularly over a period, will damage the lizard's liver.

Placing a paving stone in the feeding area provides an easily cleaned surface which may have the added benefit of keeping the lizards' nails short and reducing the risk of inadvertent substrate ingestion.

Ingestion of substrate, causing a blockage in the gut, is very common in Bearded Dragons. Admittedly, it is more common when an inappropriate diet is fed. This may occur when the vegetable material is missing and the animal attempts to eat substrate or the artificial plants which some people place in the vivarium to make it more visually pleasing.

Substrate materials that, if eaten, will pass through the gut without causing a blockage, are preferable. There will be a compromise between having a visually pleasing enclosure and using a safe substrate material.

• Newspaper works very well as a substrate, although it does not make for the most attractive-looking vivaria. It will not be inadvertently ingested, it is easily removed when soiled, and usually can be obtained free.

- Wood chippings provide the greatest risk of ingestion and blockages and should be avoided. Large size bark chippings are less likely to be ingested but, with this type of substrate, it is difficult to see the faeces and urates deposited in it, and the uneaten food and insects, all of which need to be removed.

- Sand is commonly used, although it has occasionally

been associated with gut blockages. It can be used to make a very attractive, natural-looking vivarium.

- Digestible substrates are commercially available which, if inadvertently ingested, will move through the digestive system without causing blockages. Some of these are composed of calcium carbonate so, if digested, they will also supply additional calcium to the diet.

- Some people use rabbit pellets, on the basis that they are

Newspaper provides a practical and inexpensive substrate.

A sand substrate gives a natural appearance to the vivarium.

digestible if eaten and they smell nice. However, even these substrates have occasionally been associated with blockages if the animal gorges itself on them.

- Artificial grass is also a good substrate. It can easily be removed when soiled and then washed.

- The modern trend is towards using combinations of substrates, which give the lizard some variety in the surface on which it moves. This option can also create more visually pleasing vivaria.

DECOR

A background picture with a semi-arid scene on one or two sides will enhance the appearance of the vivarium and many people are convinced that their Bearded Dragons are happier in such an enhanced environment. It can give the appearance of a much larger vivarium.

Some of these background pictures come with an insulating backing. If not, then it will help the temperature control if some insulation is improvised with some sheets of polystyrene.

Provide thick tree branches and some large boulders for the Bearded Dragons to climb on to bask. These should bring the Dragons to within 15 to 30 centimetres (6 to 12 inches) of the full spectrum light, and under the basking light where the basking temperature of 30 to 35 degrees C (86 to 95 degrees F) is achieved.

Make sure that any boulders are secure and will not roll over and injure the lizard, even if it attempts to burrow under them.

Branches also need to be securely fixed.

At the cool end, place a pile of clean, dry hay that your Dragons can burrow in when the temperatures cool down.

With the clever use of decor, you can create an attractive and realistic environment for your Bearded Dragon.

PHOTO-PERIODS

Photo-periods, which are the times when the Bearded Dragon is exposed to light, should vary through the year.

In the summer, the light should be on for between 12 and 14 hours every day. In winter, the photo-period needs to be reduced to between 10 and 12 hours. Ideally, there should be a gradual change in the photo-period through the seasons. This is especially important if breeding is to be attempted.

THERMOSTATS

A thermostat is a box of electronics. Attached to it is a temperature probe, which is positioned inside the vivarium. It is also connected to at least one of the heat sources. The thermostat is set to control the temperature (usually by a dial on the front) in the vivarium by varying the heat output from the heat source. There is a constant feedback from the temperature probe to the thermostat, allowing it to respond to temperature changes within the vivarium.

In cheaper models, the thermostat is usually connected just to a heat mat. More advanced thermostats can connect to multiple heat sources and can be programmed to change to a night-time temperature setting at a preset time.

The most advanced models will also switch the lighting on and off, thereby controlling the photo-period. Some will even simulate a period of dusk and dawn before complete darkness.

Thermostats are manufactured by many companies and are

Furnish the vivarium with a variety of branches and boulders so your Bearded Dragons have a variety of places to bask or to burrow.

available from reptile shops. Magazines devoted to reptile-keeping are also a good source of information.

THERMOMETERS

The range of temperatures achieved in different areas of the enclosure, including under the basking light and the night-time temperatures, needs to be measured.

A thermometer that is positioned halfway up the wall of the enclosure or vivarium will not give useful information about the temperature at ground level. Ideally, two thermometers, one at each end of the enclosure, should constantly monitor the enclosure temperature.

Even when a thermostat is being used to control the temperature, thermometers should still be used independently, as the thermostat may be calibrated incorrectly, or the animals may move the probe.

For example, if the probe gets pushed into the water bowl, then it will read too low a temperature and the thermostat will try to compensate by increasing the heat output, which will result in the vivarium overheating. This can quickly result in hyperthermia if the lizards do not have a cooler area to escape to, or a water bowl in which they can soak.

Hyperthermia is often fatal unless the Bearded Dragons are found early. Juvenile dragons are more susceptible to hyperthermia than adults, due to their larger surface area relative to body size.

UV LIGHT

Exposure to an ultraviolet light source is important for Bearded Dragons in order to metabolise calcium.

Full-spectrum light sources, such as the sun and the specially designed full-spectrum light tubes, in addition to providing the necessary UVB, also have a positive behavioural and psychological effect caused by the other types of light that they emit.

It is the ultraviolet B type of ultraviolet light, in the range of 280-315 nm, as provided by full-spectrum light designed for reptiles, which is required to allow the animal to use calcium.

The figure 280-315 pertains to the wavelength of the 'light' (electro magnetic radiation). EMR of different wavelengths has different effects on tissue, and some are harmful.

The term 'UV light' is loosely applied to both full-spectrum lights and also to black lights and actinics.

Black lights and actinics glow a purple colour when switched on (as opposed to white from full-spectrum tubes). Because of the danger attached to this level of UV light, protective goggles should be worn when working with them.

There are also concerns about the effect this type of lighting has on reptilian eyes and skin. Because of these dangers, and the fact that they do not provide the beneficial behaviour and psychological effect of the full-spectrum sources, black lights and actinics are no longer recommended.

UV/VITAMIN D3

When skin is exposed to ultraviolet light in the range of 280 to 315 nm, previtamin D is changed to the active form 'vitamin D3'. Vitamin D3 has the very important job of stimulating the gut to absorb the calcium present in food and also to encourage its incorporation into bones. Vitamin D3 can be provided in the food but there is a great risk of toxicity from over-supplementation.

Signs of this would include weak, poorly mineralised bones (also a sign of deficient D3), and calcium being laid down in soft tissues (blood vessels, kidneys, lungs, heart and other tissues). Death is usually the result in extreme cases. Over-exposure to ultraviolet light does not produce excess vitamin D3, for reasons which are not fully understood.

ENVIRONMENTAL CONTROL SYSTEMS

Environmental control systems are appearing on the market that will control all the heat and light sources in the enclosure or the vivarium and will also control the photo-period and the night-time drop in temperature. These systems are making environmental control a lot easier.

Exposure to natural sunlight can be very beneficial to Bearded Dragons.

SUNLIGHT

Natural sunlight is the best source of light. Even in colder climates, exposing Bearded Dragons, especially young, growing Dragons, to natural sunlight on hot days, even for just 10 to 20 minutes, is extremely valuable.

It must, however, be remembered that UVB will not penetrate through glass or plastic, so that even Dragons maintained in greenhouses will need ultraviolet light exposure (either directly from the sun or from an artificial light source).

Precautions must be taken to prevent overheating when providing exposure to natural sunlight. Adequate shade must always be provided.

FULL-SPECTRUM

If sufficient natural sunlight cannot be provided, Bearded Dragons should have full-spectrum lighting.

These are a type of commercially available fluorescent tubes specially developed for their ability to provide UVB radiation and imitate the full spectrum of the sun's visible light.

As with the sun's radiation, no glass or plastic should be between the lizard and the light. It is also important that the Dragons are within 15 to 30 centimetres (6 to 12 inches) of the bulb.

Alternatively, test kits are available to check the output of UVB radiation from the tube.

As distance from the full-spectrum light source increases, the concentration of UVB radiation decreases fourfold.

The tubes should be changed every six months, or in accordance with the manufacturer's recommendations, since UVB production diminishes even though the tubes still produce visible light.

Newer full-spectrum light sources which also produce heat are now available. This means that a basking light may not be necessary. Full-spectrum lights should be left switched on for the daytime photo-period.

OUTDOOR ENCLOSURES

Outdoor enclosures are either permanent or seasonal. Choose a site that provides shade as well as sun throughout the day. A site that looks perfect in the early morning may bake under the late afternoon sun.

Even when outside, Bearded Dragons can overheat on a hot day if no shade is available. Also, all outdoor enclosures should have a water bowl, large enough for the lizards to soak in, which they will use for temperature control. It is advisable to position the enclosure in a site where it can be seen from the windows of the house.

PROTECTION

The roof needs to be covered in wire to keep predators out, but not glass or plastic that would screen out the essential UVB part of the sun's rays, and predispose the enclosure to overheating – the greenhouse effect.

Beware of dogs, cats and other predators, and even the neighbours' kids, attempting to get into the enclosure. A strong enclosure and padlocks are strongly advisable.

In areas where, in the winter, the temperature drops below 25 degrees C (77 degrees F), supplementary heat will be needed. Ceramic heat lamps can provide this. Do not allow night-time temperatures regularly to drop below 17 degrees C (62.6 degrees F).

HUMIDITY

Outdoor enclosures are not recommended for Bearded Dragons in areas of high rainfall, unless they are set up inside covered and well-ventilated greenhouses.

As Bearded Dragons come from a relatively dry, semi-arid area, with primarily seasonal summer rains, they will not do well in damp environments.

An outdoor enclosure will be appreciated, but it is generally a seasonal option.

TEMPERATURE

A good compromise for temperate areas, which have long hot summers, is to have a large vivarium, which can be carried outside in the summer.

As a guide, if the daytime temperature in your area is, on average, between 25 to 30 degrees C (77 to 86 degrees F), and at night it does not drop below 17 degrees C (62.6 degrees F), then outdoor enclosures are ideal.

Short periods of higher temperatures for several days, or for parts of the day, will result in healthy Bearded Dragons seeking shelter for those periods and becoming inactive. This is within the normal behaviour of the species, as it would occur in its normal habitat in Australia.

Periods of environmental temperatures below 25 degrees C (77 degrees F), especially if there is no opportunity to bask (for example overcast skies), will be detrimental if prolonged, so supplementary heating should be provided. If there is the opportunity to bask, then a healthy Dragon will be able to thermo-regulate and a short period of low temperature will not cause any problems.

Depending on the ambient temperature, additional heating may or may not be required. Underfloor heating pads are an effective way of providing additional heating where necessary.

These, and any other additional heat sources, should be connected to a controlling thermostat, which has a heat probe positioned centrally in the enclosure.

In areas of the world where these temperatures are not achieved outdoors, such as in the UK, the Bearded Dragon needs to be kept indoors in a vivarium.

SOIL CARE

Care has to be taken to prevent the build-up of parasites in the soil. This can be achieved by rotating the enclosure to different areas or, if this is not possible, by removing the top layer of soil regularly.

Alternatively, outdoor carpet can be used which can be taken out and cleaned monthly. It is easiest to have a spare piece which can be rotated, to allow time to wash it properly and dry the carpet before it is replaced.

BRUMATION

In periods of adverse conditions, when it is very hot or too cold, many Bearded Dragons will go into a dormant state.

In the wild, this time is spent in burrows, under boulders or, sometimes, they dig into the ground. This is brumation. It does not involve the more extreme body changes associated with hibernation.

Bearded Dragons can be kept and bred successfully without a period of brumation. However, many owners believe (probably extrapolating from what happens in other reptile species) that a period of brumation will increase sperm count and egg viability.

If your animal goes into brumation by accident, through heat deficiency, or by design, it should fully recover when ideal environment temperatures are re-established.

If it does not quickly return to normal behaviour, that is within 24 hours, or if it has lost weight, then it should be examined by a reptile vet.

4 *Routine Care*

Bearded Dragons can become very tame, interacting well with humans, but the full range of their social abilities will only be seen if there are two or more of them together. Handling your Bearded Dragons will make them more tame as they come to trust you, and will lead to a more rewarding relationship with them. Other direct contact, such as hand-feeding them, is also important. This relationship becomes even more special as you start to interpret the meaning of some of their attempts at communication.

HANDLING

Bearded Dragons rarely bite, scratch, or whip their tails, as other lizards often do. Many appear to enjoy the warmth of human skin and like to lie on your chest with their head on your shoulder. Dragons that have developed a relationship with their owners will, if they have become agitated for some reason, often calm down when put in this position.

Dragons will not be as relaxed with strangers as they are with their owners, and often will be

The Bearded Dragon should be supported from underneath when it is being handled.

very reluctant to allow themselves to be picked up by unknown humans.

SUPPORT

When a Bearded Dragon is being lifted or carried, its body should be carefully supported from underneath. Its tail also needs to be supported, as otherwise it will feel out of balance and may thrash its tail about.

TAILS

Bearded Dragons should never be caught or lifted by their tail. Unlike some other lizard species, Bearded Dragons cannot drop their tail as a defence mechanism and, if it is bitten off, that portion of the tail will not grow back.

HARNESSES

When carrying the lizard, be aware that it might take a sudden leap away from you. Take care when carrying them around, as they do not grip on very hard and so may fall off. They may also suddenly dash off your body and injure themselves, especially if they have been startled.

A harness can be made, such as the one you can buy for iguanas, which gives increased safety while carrying them around.

If you provide branches and rocks for climbing, the nails should wear down naturally.

NAILS

The nails of the Bearded Dragon may be contaminated with faeces from walking around the enclosure. Any scratches on your skin will be contaminated. Always treat scratches seriously. Cleanse them thoroughly with antiseptic solution.

If the wound is deep and not responding to first-aid treatment, see your doctor.

NATURAL WEAR

Placing a paving stone in their feeding area provides a surface which can easily be cleaned and also helps to keep the Dragons' nails short.

Additionally, you can take advantage of their fondness for climbing up to bask. If climbed regularly, a large rock placed under the basking light will also keep the Dragons' nails short. Take care that it is stable and not liable to wobble, or roll over.

TRIMMING

If it is still necessary to trim your Dragons' nails, you can use a cat claw trimmer or a pair of human nail clippers.

It is only necessary to remove the sharp tip of each claw. Get an assistant to hold the Bearded Dragon securely for you, as jumping at the wrong time could injure it. If you cut the nail too high up where there is a small nerve and a blood vessel present, there will be some bleeding.

BLEEDING

Bleeding should stop if gentle pressure is applied to the cut surface for one to two minutes. Alternatively, a coagulating agent (such as ferric chloride or silver nitrate) can be applied. Cornflour can sometimes help if these others are not available.

In normal, healthy Bearded Dragons, any small amount of bleeding that would result from cutting a nail too short should stop either on its own or with gentle pressure.

If bleeding continues, then there may be internal medical problems that are affecting the clotting ability of the blood. These should be investigated.

HOUSE-TRAINING

It is possible to train Bearded Dragons to defecate in one specific area, such as on paper. They can even be trained to use a cat litter tray containing cat litter or other suitable absorbent material.

This minimises the cleaning necessary and helps reduce the spread of internal parasites.

House-training is easier when one or two are kept. Some individuals will defecate in one spot only without any training. Social groups in larger enclosures are more difficult to train in this way.

If a litter tray is used, then cover it with just a thin layer of whatever absorbent material you use. Deep layers of litter may have the retrograde effect of encouraging digging, which increases contact with the stools.

Place your Bearded Dragon in a sealed container while you are cleaning the vivarium.

EXERCISING

Bearded Dragons are active lizards and require a large enclosure in order to thrive. The enclosure should be large enough so that special exercising is not necessary. It is not recommended that Bearded Dragons be allowed to roam freely either in a house or a garden.

CLEANING

Cleaning the vivarium or any enclosure in which the Bearded Dragon is kept, whether it be indoor or outdoor, involves the removal of uneaten food, faeces, urates, saliva, blood and other body secretions.

When you have done that, you then need to disinfect all the surfaces. It is essential that no disease-causing agents are allowed to invade the vivarium.

Disinfectants are not effective in dirty areas. Therefore, the debris has to be removed before disinfectants can work properly.

While you are cleaning the vivarium or enclosure, the occupants can be safely secured in an easily cleaned container such as the box used for their transport or a spare vivarium.

CLEANING KIT

Assemble a cleaning kit containing all the tools required to do a good job.
- Rubber gloves
- Scrapers (paint scraper for example)
- Bucket (for hot soapy water)
- Bucket (for rinse water)
- Towels, paper or cloth
- Bag for waste
- Soap (dish-washing varieties work well)
- Disinfectant

DISINFECTANTS

This is a rapidly developing area with new chemicals being developed all the time that are safer and more effective. It is best to seek the advice of your reptile veterinarian as to the most suitable disinfectants that are locally available.

ISOLATION

Ideally, each vivarium should have its own cleaning kit. This is to minimise the spread of any disease. Where this is not possible, healthy animals should be cleaned first, and the kit must be disinfected between each group of animals.

Any animals that have any infection (proved or suspected) should have their enclosures cleaned last to reduce the risk of spreading disease.

ROUTINES

DAILY

Uneaten vegetable material should be removed at the end of each day,

with faeces and, if eaten, this will otherwise it may become soiled result in an increase of internal parasites with a direct life cycle.

Additionally, food left in the warm vivarium will perish rapidly, having reduced water content and potentially building up high levels of fungal toxins.

Escaped crickets and other insects need also to be removed. If they remain within the enclosure, they may feed on the faeces of the Bearded Dragons, increasing the risk of building up the parasite burden. Occasionally, they may start to chew on the Bearded Dragons, especially at night and if no other food is available.

Insects that have been present in the vivarium for longer than one hour are of reduced food value due to the fact that their guts will be empty.

All uneaten food must be removed from the vivarium.

43

Faeces should be removed daily, together with the substrate surrounding it. Bearded Dragon faecal pellets are generally firm rather than runny and so are easily removed with a cat litter scoop.

Food and water pots should also be cleaned daily. Soapy hot water is the best medium to wash these in, making sure that all suds are rinsed away.

MONTHLY

Monthly (depending on the size and number of individuals present) all the cage furniture, such as rocks and basking branches, should be removed to be washed in soapy water and then disinfected.

The substrate should be replaced at this time also. If the enclosure is lined with Astroturf or outdoor carpet, then it is best to have a second piece so that plenty of time is available to clean, disinfect and dry the soiled piece.

The walls should also be cleaned and disinfected if they come into contact with animal secretions or food items. Mixing half a litre of rubbing alcohol with 50 millilitres of vinegar and a teaspoonful of liquid soap makes a safe glass cleaner (that is about a pint with three dessert spoons of vinegar).

Add one part of this mix to four parts water and just spray on glass or plastic and wipe as usual.

HALF-YEARLY

Outdoor enclosures, which use the ground as the substrate, should have the top 6 centimetres (2.4 inches) removed every six months, or more frequently if many animals are kept together.

SALMONELLA ALERT

Salmonella is a type of bacteria, which is the most recognised disease of reptiles transmissible to man. There are more than 2,000 types known. Not all cause disease, and some only cause disease in specific species of animal.

In humans, salmonella is most commonly caught through eating contaminated food. The types of salmonella that reptiles can carry only account for a very small percentage of human cases of salmonella. However, this could grow as the number of people in direct contact with reptiles increases, if precautions are not taken.

Salmonella infection can vary in severity from individual to individual. Symptoms vary from none, to mild flu for 24 hours,

It is essential to adopt a strict hygiene regime when keeping reptiles.

right through to extreme cases with diarrhoea, dehydration, stomach cramps, high fever and, in rare cases, even death.

As different studies estimate the incidence of salmonella in lizards to be somewhere between 13 to 41 per cent, it is safest to work on the basis that all lizards are carriers. Remember that reptiles, even though they can be infected with salmonella, rarely show any symptoms associated with that infection. Some people theorise that, in a proportion of reptiles, salmonella is a normal inhabitant of the gut.

Work is being done to develop better tests to identify the individuals that are carrying salmonella and also to develop ways to eliminate the salmonella from those carriers.

HYGIENE

There are a number of hygienic precautions to prevent salmonella and other possible diseases that might be transmissible to man.

- Do always wash hands thoroughly with soap and water after handling any reptile, cage, or cage accessories.
- Do keep reptiles out of kitchens and away from any surfaces where food for human consumption is prepared or stored.
- Do wear gloves while cleaning the reptile enclosure or during changing the water bowl.
- Do keep the reptile enclosure as clean as possible.
- Do avoid splashes to the face while cleaning the reptile enclosure by wearing eye and face protection if necessary.
- Do cover any cuts or sores with

dressings or gloves during handling.

- Do supervise children under 12 when they are handling reptiles.
- Do teach children to wash their hands thoroughly after handling.
- Do not eat, drink or smoke while handling any reptile.
- Do not put your hand in your mouth or use your mouth to hold anything (for example a writing pen) at the same time as handling any reptile.
- Do not clean reptile accessories or cage furniture in a kitchen sink.

AT RISK

The following categories of people should avoid all contact (direct or indirect) with Bearded Dragons and other reptiles, as they are the members of society most at risk of salmonella.

- Children up to the age of five.
- Anyone with HIV infection or any other immuno-suppressive illness.
- Anyone who is on any drug or treatment that suppresses the immune system.
- Pregnant women.

5 *Diet And Feeding*

Bearded Dragons are omnivorous, which means they will eat both plant and animal food sources. It is known that, in the wild, the diet of an adult Bearded Dragon probably consists of approximately 90 per cent vegetable material, whereas juveniles are truly omnivorous, feeding on 50 per cent plant material and 50 per cent animal material.

PLANTS

Vegetable material fed to Bearded Dragons should be predominantly of the dark-green leafy varieties, including:

- parsley
- spinach
- dandelions
- mustard greens
- coriander
- carrot greens
- turnip greens
- collard greens
- bok choy
- watercress
- leaves and florets from any of the cabbage family (for example, cauliflower, broccoli, kale)
- carrots, peas, beans and squash can be offered in smaller quantities
- frozen vegetables must be thoroughly thawed first.

Flowers are also good to eat, especially flowers from the plants already recommended as food plants:

- dandelion
- mustard flowers
- squash
- hibiscus
- carnations
- clover
- nasturtiums
- daisies.

LIVE FOOD

Crickets should be the primary

Cabbage, cauliflower, broccoli and kale are all recommended.

Crickets should be the primary insect that is fed.

Dandelion (left) and clover (right) will be appreciated.

Wax moth larvae can be fed in smaller quantities.

Locusts are relished by many Bearded Dragons.

insects fed, but mealworms, giant mealworms and wax moth larvae can also be supplied, but in smaller amounts.

Hard-bodied invertebrates that require longer periods of chewing should also be included (see dental disease). Examples include grasshoppers, beetles and cockroaches.

PREPARATION

Correct care of insects is very important if they are to be nutritious food for your Bearded Dragons. When purchased from the supplier, they may have had a period of water and food deprivation. Often, in the few days after they are purchased, a

percentage will die as a result of this deprivation.

When they arrive home, have a separate vivarium set up for them. Room temperature is adequate. No special heating or lighting is necessary. To make it easier to keep clean, be minimalist with the cage furniture, just a small log to climb up on is enough. Make sure to remove any dead crickets as soon as they are noticed.

Provide water in a shallow dish that they can easily access, but also fill it with cotton wool (cotton) to prevent them drowning.

The insects should be provided with a complete animal ration such as dry dog food, dry cat food, primate chow or rodent chow. Complete insectivore diets such as hedgehog food, or sugar glider food, can also be used.

Make sure that they can eat the dry food, as some of these diets are very hard and may need to be crumbled. Complete insect foods, designed to be fed as the sole diet for insects destined as food for other animals, are now available and these foods result in the most nutritious insects and, if available, should be used as the sole food for the crickets.

So-called gut loading foods are designed for insects on incomplete diets to fill their guts with nutrients just before feeding them to the lizards. However, they are not very palatable and may not be eaten. The complete insect foods, if available, are preferable.

Dusting the crickets or other insect food with a high calcium, phosphorus-free supplement before feeding can further increase their food value. Place the crickets to be fed in a small plastic bag and then dust them with the supplement, gently shake and feed immediately to the Dragons.

It is very important to follow the instructions on the packaging, as the quantities to be used will vary with the concentration of the supplement. Dusting insect food should not be relied upon as the only means of supplementation. Much of it will either fall off or be cleaned off by the insect before it is eaten.

Insects contain very little calcium in their bodies. They do not have bones. Their skeleton is outside their body (an exoskeleton) and is made up of chitin, a horny material that is indigestible. Hence insect eaters very often have problems due to a shortage of calcium. The gut loading foods, complete insect foods and dusting supplements are all attempts to overcome this.

DANGERS

If foraging in the wild for insects to feed, care needs to be exercised, as not all insects are safe for your Bearded Dragon to eat.

- Fireflies, for example, contain toxins called lucibufagins that are poisonous to Bearded Dragons. The ingestion of just one can be fatal. If you live in an area of the world where these insects are present, they can also pose a risk if your Bearded Dragons live in outdoor enclosures.
- Do not collect wild insects from anywhere that may have been

Dusting the insect with a calcium supplement will help to increase the food value.

sprayed with insecticides, as these will be harmful to your Bearded Dragon, especially if it accumulates small amounts from many insects, which can result in high body levels of toxins. This is why the predator population at the top of the food chain is more affected, long-term, by these harmful chemicals than the lower target species.

• Never feed a dead insect to your Bearded Dragons, as you do not know what it has died from.

FORMULATED DIETS

As has happened with other commonly-kept species, complete diets are appearing on the market designed to replace the insect and vegetable component of the diet and to be fed exclusively. They are available in juvenile and adult formulations.

Several trials of these foods in juvenile lizards, the age group where nutrition is more challenging and negative effects of dietary manipulation are easier to identify, have shown that the brands tested performed at least as well as a conventionally fed control group.

As it may be difficult to verify the quality of the brand available to you, currently the best advice is to use these foods as an adjunct to the conventional diet and that it should not make up more than 70 per cent of the diet. The nutritional quality and the palatability will vary from brand to brand.

Palatability problems, which may be an individual rather than a group problem, can usually be overcome by mixing the formulated diet with pureed vegetables or other favoured foods and, over time, decreasing the proportion of pureed vegetables until the formulated diet is being eaten on its own.

Older Bearded Dragons may not recognise formulated diets as food. This problem can also be overcome by mixing the feed with pureed vegetables.

These formulated diets (assuming a quality brand is being used) are an easy way of providing a complete balanced diet. If they comprise 70 per cent of the diet, then additional vitamin and mineral supplements are not necessary and indeed may result in potentially harmful excesses.

MICE

Pinkies are newborn mice. They are sold frozen in reptile pet shops. Fuzzies are at the next stage and are just starting to grow their fur, hence the name. Both can be offered as food to adult Bearded Dragons instead of the insect food. Pinkies and fuzzies must be fully defrosted at room temperature before being fed.

They are nutritionally more complete, especially the fuzzies. Once a week for adult Bearded Dragons is enough. They have a much better calcium/phosphorus balance than insects. Juveniles

from five months of age will manage pinkies, which can be given twice weekly until the Dragons are fully grown.

ADULTS

Dark-green leafy vegetables should be offered freely. Chop or shred the leaves and then spray them with water prior to feeding. A calcium/vitamin supplement can then be sprinkled on top, taking care to follow instructions and not to over-supplement.

Other vegetables as detailed above can be fed as up to 30 per cent of the diet.

Chop or shred the vegetable leaves before feeding.

INSECTS/MICE

Insect food should be offered two to three times a week.

The insects should be in the bottom of a large, deep, feed bowl. You do not want them to escape and then survive for prolonged periods in the furniture of the enclosure. Make sure that the bowl is heavy enough so that it will not be tipped over as the Dragon is feeding.

Insects do provide some behavioural enrichment if they are loose in the enclosure, as the Bearded Dragons have to forage to find them.

The main disadvantage, however, is that, if they are eaten after some time, they will not be as nutritious, as their guts will be empty and body reserves of energy may be used up.

They may also have eaten some of the Bearded Dragon faeces, thus increasing internal parasite numbers.

Pinkies or fuzzies can be used instead of insect food, but need only be fed once a week.

WATER

Water should be fresh and clean and always available. It is best to use a large dish that the lizards can easily climb into.

JUVENILES

Juveniles should be offered greens and vegetables freely, as described for adults.

INSECTS

Appropriately-sized crickets (and other insects) should be offered twice daily. Uneaten crickets should be removed after an hour. By this stage, the crickets' guts will be empty and they will be of a reduced food value to the Bearded Dragons.

Also, if left in, the hungry insects may begin to feed on the Bearded Dragons, nibbling at their skin. If a Dragon is lethargic, they may cause wounds.

As juveniles are growing rapidly, the negative effects of a poor diet are much more quickly seen.

WATER

Clean and fresh water should always be available in a very shallow container. The lizards should be able to sit in the water or run through it.

HATCHLINGS

After hatching, Bearded Dragons should feed within 24 hours.

Fresh, finely-chopped leafy vegetables misted with water should be available daily. It is very

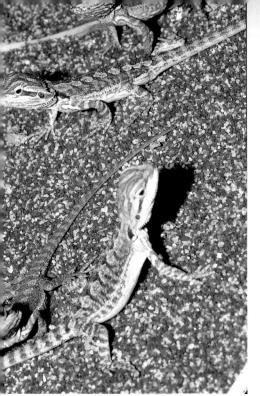
Hatchlings will need feeding within 24 hours.

important that Dragons become accustomed to eating greens. A calcium and vitamin supplement should be dusted on to the salad.

INSECTS

Two- to three-week-old crickets should be offered twice daily. They should be no bigger than the width of the hatchling's head. As they grow, the proportion of crickets decreases and the proportion of greens increases.

WATER

The water requirements are the same as for juveniles (see above).

FUSSY EATERS

It is not uncommon to encounter adult Bearded Dragons that will not eat their greens.

Often this situation develops because, at some time in the past, they were not fed an appropriate diet. They need to eat greens to achieve the balance of nutrients that will keep them healthy.

Fussy eaters can often be encouraged to eat greens by placing a bowl of chopped-up greens in their feeding area with a few wax worms or mealworms burrowing through it. Place a few more worms on the top and allow the Bearded Dragon to see them. They will eat the ones on top and look for others in the greens.

Often, by eating others that have by mistake burrowed more deeply, they will take in some greens and discover that they are actually good to eat.

Some fussy eaters are put off eating greens because of a faecally-contaminated bowl. In these cases, just make sure that the bowl is cleaned properly daily.

SUPPLEMENTS

Traditionally, vitamin and mineral supplements were very important. Nowadays it is possible, with current knowledge on nutrition, to

Try hiding a few wax worms among the greens to tempt a fussy feeder.

rear and breed Bearded Dragons successfully without using vitamin and mineral supplements.

However, the nutritional content of vegetable material varies greatly depending on how it is grown and the length of time between harvesting and eating, so it is still wise to use supplements.

Care does need to be taken not to over-supplement. Ideally the amount of supplementation given should depend on the level of deficiency in the diet.

In the real world, an estimation has to be made of the amount needed and it is usually based on the weight of the animal. Any supplement purchased should list the expiry date, a detailed break-down of the vitamin and mineral content, as well as guidelines on the level of the supplement that the manufacturers advise as suitable for a stated weight of animal.

BALANCE

Suitable supplements for Bearded Dragons should contain calcium, vitamin D3 and vitamin A. The most common nutritional deficiency seen in Bearded Dragons is an imbalance in the calcium:phosphorus ratio. Many diets contain too high a level of phosphorus and insufficient calcium.

The ratio to aim for in the diet is a minimum of 2:1 calcium: phosphorus, but the diet in the wild may contain a ratio of up to 5:1.

Many supplements sold as suitable for Bearded Dragons have a calcium:phosphorus balance of 2:1. These supplements will never correct the most common nutritional imbalance, which is calcium deficiency and phosphorus excess.

Therefore, only use supplements that contain little or no phosphorus.

If a complete formulated diet is being fed exclusively, then no supplements are necessary.

6 Breeding And Rearing

Many owners of Bearded Dragons with enough space will want to breed their animals. Indeed, if the animals are kept in ideal conditions, they will themselves want to breed. If the environmental conditions and diet are not satisfactory, then breeding will be unsuccessful.

The initial studies on breeding the species helped to work out the ideal environmental conditions and diet and establish a sound framework of husbandry knowledge. Breeding of Bearded Dragons is now well established, to the extent that the different colour morphs could be called 'breeds of Bearded Dragon'.

For the animal, breeding is normal behaviour and, by providing the optimum environment, the animal is allowed to behave completely naturally, following all its instincts which would include breeding. Of course, if space is limited, or if there would be problems rehoming the offspring, then breeding should be controlled.

Females do not need the presence of a male in order to produce eggs. Obviously, if they have not been mated, then the eggs will be infertile. However, they still need to be provided with suitable nesting sites. Gravid females (females carrying eggs) without access to a suitable nesting site, are at risk of becoming egg-bound.

SEXUAL MATURITY

A Bearded Dragon is ready to breed at 15 months. However, this can be achieved much earlier, even in Bearded Dragons as young as six months, depending on their growth rate and size. Sexual maturity usually occurs when a Bearded Dragon reaches a length of 30 to 40 centimetres (12 to 16 inches) and so the breeding age is related to body size.

The typical throat display of a mature Bearded Dragon.

NESTS

Various different nesting materials and site constructions can be successfully used, including garden soil, damp sand, a sand and peat mixture, or moist mulch.

A nesting area should be created in the vivarium within seven days of mating, by placing the appropriate material in a depression and padding it down well, to bind it. A depth of 30 centimetres (12 inches) is recommended as a minimum. Creating starter burrows to entice the females to dig will particularly help the naive animals.

PREPARATION

ENVIRONMENT

Breeding will be more successful if the environment in which the Bearded Dragons are kept replicates the normal seasonal temperature and light variations that are the trigger factors for breeding.

In the Northern hemisphere it is best to start the pre-breeding conditioning in early December. Over the following two to three weeks, the temperature is reduced so that the basking areas are approximately 25 degrees C (77 degrees F), while other areas will be significantly cooler. In the Southern hemisphere, start in early June.

Simultaneously, the photo-period is gradually reduced to 10 hours of daylight per day. If 14 hours of daylight, created by the vivarium's lighting, is the starting point, then the light should be switched off 15 minutes earlier every day until it is on for just 10 hours (which means a 10-hour photo-period) a day.

Six to eight weeks later, the heating is brought back to normal, ideally over a two-week period and, simultaneously, the photo-period is increased to 14 hours of daylight and 10 hours of darkness, reversing the process made 6 to 8 weeks earlier.

Breeding behaviour should start to be seen three to four weeks later. Many Bearded Dragons will

Temperature and light variations are the triggers for breeding.

successfully breed without the cooling period.

It is important that the enclosure is large enough, with multiple feeding stations and basking areas, or the dominant male will deny the others access.

THE ANIMALS

Bearded Dragons which are expected to breed successfully, and to lay a normal number of eggs with a hatching rate greater than 80 per cent, need to be in excellent body condition and free from any infections. A pre-breeding health check by your reptile vet is recommended.

BREEDING

In enclosures where there are two or more males housed together, intense fighting and aggressive displays will be seen as individuals attempt to establish dominance.

The males, especially the most dominant ones, will head-bob and chase females. They will also bite and attempt to carry females around by the skin on the back of their head and shoulders prior to copulation.

Females will arm wave, display and be receptive to males. Females need to be watched in case they exhibit excessive trauma to the skin on the back of their head and shoulders.

LAYING

Clutch sizes usually number from 15 to 25 eggs. However, they may range from six to 40. Females will typically lay from three to five clutches of eggs, spaced between two to five weeks, during the breeding season.

In their first year of breeding, they will usually produce three clutches of eggs, with up to seven clutches being produced in the second year. From the third year of breeding onwards, the number of clutches will begin to drop.

SUPPLEMENTS

Egg production at such an intensive level places a high demand on the female. Even with excellent diets, calcium supplementation is highly recommended.

Females must be monitored closely for loss of body condition. For the first few days following egg laying, a female may need to be fed by hand to ensure that she recovers adequately.

NESTING

Females generally lay their eggs two to three weeks after being

A pregnant Bearded Dragon: Suitable nesting areas must be provided.

mated. Post-mating and prior to laying, females begin to show abdominal enlargement, and possibly loss of muscle mass, especially along the spine and the limbs of the body.

Prior to egg laying, the females will be restless and digging in various sites as they search for a suitable nesting area.

It is essential that a suitable nesting area be provided, as detailed above. If they do not locate a suitable nesting area, many females will be reluctant to lay their eggs and may become egg-bound.

The nesting burrows constructed by the Bearded Dragons are generally of such a depth that, during egg laying, only the tip of the female's head will be visible at the entrance of the burrow.

MATERNITY

Most reptiles show no maternal care of their eggs or offspring beyond choosing an appropriate nesting site and concealing the eggs.

Bearded Dragons are no exception. Indeed, the hatchlings have to be housed separately from the adult parents for their own safety. This is why the preparation of the incubator and the hatchling area is so important.

INCUBATORS

Preparation for incubation of the eggs prior to laying is important. An incubator needs to be prepared to maintain the eggs at a temperature of 29 degrees C (84.2 degrees F). It needs to be set up and calibrated in the incubation room for at least 24 hours before it is needed, in order to make sure

The eggs will need to be transferred to an incubator.

that it maintains the required temperature.

The temperature of the incubator should be readable without having to open it. If the incubator temperature varies from its setting, then there should be an alarm to allow immediate action to be taken to rectify it.

POSITION

The incubator should, ideally, be in a small room where it is easy to maintain a steady temperature. The room's temperature needs to be cooler than the incubator, as incubators do not cool and high temperatures are more likely to damage the eggs than cooler ones.

There should be a maximum and minimum thermometer and a humidity meter in the room so

extreme fluctuations in temperature are recorded. Summer heat waves pose the greatest risk.

SUBSTRATE

Various substrates have been used for incubation. Good results have been obtained using five parts vermiculite to four parts water by weight. Vermiculite is a natural product. It is made from micaschist, which is a natural rock that is expanded in a vacuum under high temperature. It is widely available in reptile pet shops.

Vermiculite is recommended as it is clean and free from the bacteria and fungi that could damage the eggs. The vermiculite should not be allowed to dry out.

INCUBATION

After the female has completed her egg laying, you must carefully dig the eggs up and remove them from the egg-laying site, keeping them the same way up.

The eggs should then be buried two-thirds down into the vermiculite. It is easier to place the vermiculite in a small plastic box with air holes poked in it to allow some air exchange and then place the entire box into the incubator.

Unlike bird eggs, reptile eggs should not be turned during incubation. Turning will result in the death of the embryos.

The eggs will usually hatch after 50 to 70 days. Individual clutches usually hatch over a two- to three-day period. Occasionally, some eggs may hatch as long as a week later.

HATCHLINGS

Once hatchlings have left their shell, they can be placed in a separate box lined with moist paper towels and kept in the incubator for a day or two while the rest of the clutch hatches.

The hatchlings should be examined for any abnormalities. Problems with absorption of the yolk sac are not uncommon.

Any abnormalities should be reported to a reptile vet as soon as possible.

The hatchling will break its way out of the shell.

The hatchlings should be moved to a small, rearing vivarium.

REARING

When the hatchlings are removed from the incubator, they are placed in a small rearing vivarium which is, essentially, a smaller version of the adult vivarium.

Bearded Dragons must be housed by size. Smaller specimens are in danger of having parts of their tails and their toes nipped off. Also, they will often be denied access to food by dominant larger Dragons.

For the first week, use sheets of paper or kitchen towel as a substrate.

TEMPERATURE

Environmental temperature is crucial for hatchlings. They are much more sensitive to temperature deviations outside their normal range, which is 25 to 30 degrees C (77 to 86 degrees F) ambient daytime temperature, with a basking temperature of 30 to 35 degrees C (86 to 95 degrees F). Do not allow the night-time temperature to drop below 22 degrees C (71.6 degrees F) for hatchlings.

DIET

Hatchlings need to be observed to ensure that they are all eating and basking. At this stage, if they do not eat, they will quickly become dehydrated.

- Fresh, finely-chopped, leafy vegetables misted with water should be available daily. It is very important that the hatchlings become accustomed to eating greens.

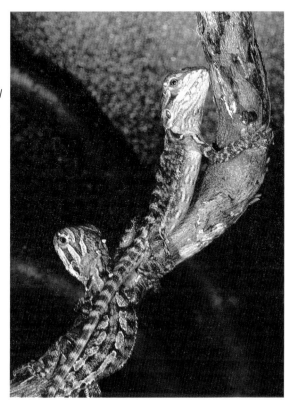

Keep a close check on all the hatchlings to ensure they are feeding properly.

- A calcium and vitamin supplement should be dusted on to the salad.
- Two- to three-week-old crickets should be offered twice daily.
- The crickets should be no bigger than the width of the hatchling's head.
- As the hatchlings grow, the proportion of crickets eaten will decrease and the proportion of greens increases.

REHOMING

If the hatchlings are moving on to a new owner immediately, do ensure that they will be cared for appropriately. At this age they are at their most vulnerable, so give clear written instructions.

7 *Health Care*

Sick Bearded Dragons all look alike. Regardless of the cause, a sick Dragon tends to be mentally dull, inactive and off its food. If these signs are seen, then you need to seek the advice of a vet, and preferably one who knows about reptiles.

VETERINARIANS

Once you have decided to keep Bearded Dragons, you should register with a reptilian veterinarian.

In many countries, vets can pursue further qualifications in exotic and zoological animal medicine, qualifications which ensure that they have the knowledge necessary for reptile medicine and surgery. It also makes it more likely that they will have the necessary diagnostic, hospitalisation and surgical equipment on hand.

In many areas of the world, it will not be possible to find vets with specialist qualifications. If this is the case, then seek out a local vet who is interested in treating reptiles and who will be able to consult with more knowledgeable colleagues further afield if a difficult case is encountered.

INTERNET INFO

The Association of Reptilian and Amphibian Veterinarians is a non-profit-making international organisation with the aim of improving reptilian and amphibian veterinary care and husbandry worldwide through education, exchange of ideas and research.

Its website gives information about its membership lists, which is another way of locating veterinarians interested in treating reptiles. The web site address is HYPERLINK http://www.arav.org. This website is also a useful source of information with links to other reptilian web sites.

COMMON AILMENTS

DENTAL DISEASE

Bearded Dragons have the type of teeth called acrodontic dentition. They are not replaced throughout life, like the teeth of most other types of reptiles.

Dental disease is quite common in captive Bearded Dragons. Diets comprising crickets, mealworms and fruit lead more quickly to plaque accumulation and periodontal disease. Diets incorporating more hard-bodied beetles and cockroaches increase the length of time that the Dragon has to chew on them, which dramatically reduces the incidence of periodontal disease.

Dental disease is not found in wild lizards, which eat a much wider variety of food items, both plant and insect, and include items which require a lot more chewing, resulting in improved oral hygiene.

If periodontal disease is already present, then a veterinarian should see your lizard. Often the disease is much deeper than is first realised. Treatment will depend on whether it is bacterial or fungal, and of which type. Usually a deep sample needs to be taken and grown in the lab. This is then tested against different antibiotics or antifungal drugs.

If the infection is very deep, then surgery may be needed to remove the bulk of the infected bone, followed by the appropriate antifungicide or antibiotic (or sometimes a mixture).

The Bearded Dragon retains the same set of teeth throughout its life.

The frequency of skin shedding depends on growth rate.

It must be remembered that infection will sometimes get into the blood stream and spread to distant sites within the body. These develop into internal abscesses and can be very difficult to detect.

Looking at the blood cells may give some clues, but internal samples taken by endoscopy, or exploratory surgery, may be necessary if the dental disease is cured but the Dragon is still unwell.

MOUTH ROT

This is inflammation of the mouth. The Dragon is often predisposed to this by some underlying disease or nutritional deficiency that reduces its immunity. Stomatitis is a more correct term for this. In Bearded Dragons, it may also be an extension of dental disease, as detailed above. Treatment involves correction of the cause. Antibiotics are often also necessary.

SHEDDING

Dysectysis is the technical term for problems in shedding. Bearded Dragons, like all lizards, shed their skins in pieces, unlike snakes that shed it in one piece. The frequency of shedding depends on

the Dragon's growth rate. Rapidly-growing juveniles may shed every two weeks. On areas of skin where there are scars, or if the animal is dehydrated, then there will be problems with shedding.

Increasing the humidity may help temporarily, but the cause of the dehydration, or underlying skin problems, should be investigated.

PARASITES

INTERNAL

Bearded Dragons are particularly susceptible to parasitism. While extremely animated and personable, Bearded Dragons are sloppy and think nothing of plodding through their faeces, food and water dish. This results in their food and water becoming faecally contaminated, with a resultant increase in the types of internal parasites that have a direct life cycle.

The commonest parasites found in Bearded Dragons are coccidia and pinworms. Flagellates are also commonly found. These and other internal parasites can only be diagnosed by examining a faecal sample under the microscope. Some parasites need special staining to be identified.

Different parasites are spread in different ways, and the drug required to eliminate the parasite and any husbandry changes depends on which parasite is being treated. Therefore, it is essential to identify which parasites are present and to verify afterwards that the treatment was successful.

COCCIDIA

Coccidia are single-cell organisms that live in the lining of the intestine. Bearded Dragons have their own species, *Isosporo amphibulori*, which is a common cause of disease. Small infestations may not cause any symptoms; however, when there are large numbers present, the Bearded Dragon will be mentally dull, inactive, dehydrated and not eating.

Coccidial infections will predispose the Bearded Dragon to other problems, for example, dietary deficiencies (due to malabsorption e.g. hypocalcaemia) and adenovirus infection.

They are diagnosed by microscopic examination of a prepared stool sample at a magnification of 400 times. It is the oocyst, a form of the organism shed in the stool, which is enclosed in a resistant wall, that is seen under the microscope.

The oocyst then turns into an infective form, usually over several days. If eaten, this will infect the lizard. Alternatively, if the stools are eaten by an insect, this will infect any lizard which then eats that insect.

Unclean enclosures can result in very heavy infections that can become life-threatening. The traditional treatment was with sulphonamide drugs. Care has to be taken with the use of these drugs in dehydrated animals. There are newer drugs being developed which are showing promise in the treatment of coccidial infections in reptiles.

It is always wise to check a stool sample after treatment to confirm that the parasite has been eliminated.

PINWORMS

Oxyurids (pinworms) are nearly as common as coccidia. They are worms that live in the intestine. Sometimes they are referred to as nematodes. Some veterinarians believe that they may play a useful role in mixing the gut contents and so aid digestion. They are certainly not necessary for normal digestion as they are not always present.

Large infections of pinworms will cause large bowel irritation, impactions in the intestines and rectal prolapses. They also have a direct life cycle, with the eggs (more correctly referred to as ova) being passed in the stools, which can directly infect the Bearded Dragon, by ingestion.

They are also diagnosed by microscopic examination of a prepared stool sample at a magnification of 400 times. There are many different drugs used to treat oxyurids depending on what part of the world you are in. Most of the drugs used to treat pinworm infestations are given by mouth.

Again, it is best practice to check a stool sample after treatment to confirm that the parasite has been eliminated. Do note that these are not the same pinworms that infect humans.

FLAGELLATES

Flagellates are single-cell organisms that move around in a whip-like fashion, using one or more long, mobile, whip-like appendages called flagella. There are many different types, and most are harmless in small numbers. In very large numbers they may cause dehydration and diarrhoea, or just the non-specific signs of a sick Dragon which is mentally dull, inactive and off its food.

Again, preferred treatments vary in different parts of the world, often relying on which drugs are available. Metronidazole and fenbendazole are two drugs commonly used in flagellate infections. These drugs are given by mouth.

Detection is usually by making a

direct smear of fresh, still warm stool sample, as flagellates die off quickly in the sample. Some flagellates form spores, which can be detected in older samples prepared as for coccidia and oxyurids.

TAPEWORMS

Tapeworms are not that common, as they need an intermediate host in their life cycle. The tapeworm 'egg' has to be eaten by an insect. Once inside the insect's body, it develops further, so that when a Bearded Dragon eats the insect, it will then be able to complete its life cycle and develop into an adult tapeworm in the Bearded Dragon.

There are also types of tapeworms that use rodents as their intermediate host. Feeding wild-caught pinkies (newborn mice) will, therefore, carry the risk of infecting the Bearded Dragons with tapeworms.

Heavy infestations will result in weight loss and dehydration. Appetite may be increased and there is often irritation in the large bowel.

Usually detection is easy, because the tapeworm segments are visible to the naked eye on the stools. Heavy infestations will produce large numbers of segments. However, segments are not always present. They are often passed intermittently.

The segments are full of eggs. Sometimes, tapeworm eggs, which are much larger than oxyurid eggs, are seen by microscopic examination of a prepared stool

sample. Currently the preferred treatment is praziquentel, which is usually effective.

PENTASTOMIDS

Pentastomids are internal parasites with a complex life cycle. The adult pentastomid lives in the lungs of the Bearded Dragon. They are rare in captive Bearded Dragons.

There is no known effective treatment at present. Infections are without major signs and most of the damage is done when the larvae of the pentastomid is migrating. This parasite can potentially infect man.

MICROSPORIDIA

Microsporidia are single-celled parasites with an unusual life cycle. They have only rarely been reported in Bearded Dragons. No confirmed cases have survived.

If the infection is diagnosed in a living animal, there is currently no known effective cure. Transmission is unknown but may be from infected carriers. It is also speculated that insect food may be a source of the infection.

OTHER PARASITES

Other parasites which are known to occur in various reptile species from different parts of the world could easily infect Bearded Dragons, so avoid mixing different species of reptile, especially when they come from different continents. Also, if your Bearded

Dragons are housed in an outdoor enclosure, then try to keep native lizards and snakes out, as well as potential intermediate hosts.

EXTERNAL

Bearded Dragons can occasionally pick up mites from other lizards. Sometimes these can be removed by just bathing the Dragon in water. Sometimes insecticides are necessary.

Do not use organophosphates, as these are very toxic. These are often sold as insect pest strips and, even though they are commonly recommended by herpetologists, they are a common cause of death in reptiles. It is best to identify the mite first so that a plan can be worked out for eradication based on its life cycle.

You must talk to your reptile veterinarian about any skin problems in your Dragons.

TREMORS

Twitching, tremors or seizures are all symptoms which can be related to poisons such as insecticides, infections involving the nervous system, or a variety of internal medical problems such as kidney, parathyroid and liver problems. Low blood calcium can also result in muscle tremors.

These symptoms are the sign of potentially serious underlying disease and require immediate veterinary investigation. Usually a blood sample is urgently needed to reach a diagnosis before treatment can be started. It is risky to give calcium on the assumption that the

symptoms might be due to low calcium.

If phosphorus blood levels are very high, then giving extra calcium may tip the solubility balance and the minerals will crystallize out in the blood vessels, causing the death of the lizard.

With a blood sample, the levels of calcium and phosphorus in the blood can be measured and the solubility index can be calculated. If calcium is low and the phosphorus high, then injected fluids will have to be given first to bring phosphorus levels down before calcium can be safely given.

BREATHING

Sometimes Bearded Dragons with respiratory infections will be seen to have laboured breathing or to have a discharge from the nares. More commonly, the only symptoms noticed may be loss of appetite, lethargy and weight loss.

Investigations into the cause will probably include culturing some of the secretions to try to identify the disease-causing agent.

If a bacterium or a fungus is identified, then the laboratory will usually test it against different drugs to check which will kill it and which ones it is resistant to. This allows an appropriate drug to

be chosen for treatment.

The secretions for testing need to be taken from deep in the airways, as otherwise the laboratory may just end up testing a bacterium or fungus that was picked up on the outside of the Dragon and which is a normal inhabitant of the skin or nose cavities and is not the causative agent.

Endoscopy allows the vet to look inside the lungs and take samples from deep inside if necessary. Lung washes are another way of obtaining samples from deep inside the lungs, if sufficiently small endoscopes are not available.

EGG-BINDING

A healthy Bearded Dragon on a good diet, kept at the correct temperatures and with appropriate nesting sites available, is unlikely to have egg-laying problems.

A diagnosis of egg-binding is made when a breeding female is seen to be straining and has been noticed digging. Sometimes, a radiograph or an ultrasound scan may be necessary to reach a dignosis. Occasionally, further tests are necessary to establish a cause.

Where environmental causes have been ruled out, or where environmental corrective changes

have failed to rectify the egg-binding (such as provision of suitable nesting sites and ensuring that the vivaria are at the correct temperatures), then the help of a reptile veterinarian should be sought before the animal's condition becomes irreversible.

DIARRHOEA

The most common causes are internal parasites (most commonly, coccidia, oxyurids or flagellates), bacterial and viral causes, and inappropriate food. Examination of a sample for bacteria and parasites is necessary to decide on the best treatment.

If the Dragon is dehydrated, then intra-osseous fluids may be necessary, along with the appropriate treatment for the cause. In less severe cases, fluids can be given by mouth.

Do not use liquid feeding products designed for humans, dogs or cats in Bearded Dragons, especially if they already have diarrhoea. These products will very often cause diarrhoea in healthy Bearded Dragons and may predispose them to gout.

DEHYDRATION

Dehydrated animals often need fluids urgently to stop their

circulatory system from failing. In man, and in most domesticated mammals, fluids can be given directly into a vein, through an intra-venous drip.

In small reptiles this is not possible, due to their size and also because of their skin type and the non-availability of easily accessible veins.

However, they, of course, can have the same life-threatening situations, where fluids directly entering into their circulation are essential for survival.

In these situations, fluids are given directly into the bone marrow via a catheter from where they immediately flow into the blood vessels. This is called intra-osseous fluids and, as with intra-venous drips, the flow of fluid is controlled by an infusion pump.

WOUNDS

Usually these are inflicted by other animals. You can clean superficial wounds with appropriate antiseptic solutions (e.g. povodine iodine is widely available under a variety of trade names).

Your reptile veterinarian will be

able to advise on what locally available antiseptics are useful and on the correct dilution and frequency of use. Deeper wounds may need suturing and/or antimicrobial drugs. You need to consult your reptile vet.

BURNS

These usually occur when a Bearded Dragon, attempting to warm itself, snuggles up to a heating element or a hot bulb. The area of the burn may not be noticed until many days later when the dead skin eventually sloughs.

These affected areas are usually much deeper than they appear and frequently become infected. In these cases, there is a high risk of life-threatening blood poisoning. Consult the vet as soon as you suspect a burn has occurred.

FRACTURES

All bone fractures are painful. Management of bone fractures depends on the cause and any underlying factors. Bearded Dragons with broken bones need to be seen by a reptile veterinarian.

If the end of the broken bone has penetrated the skin, it will be infected and will need cleaning and appropriate antibiotics. The fracture may need to be immobilised by external bandaging or by surgery to facilitate healing.

Some fractures will heal without immobilisation of the fracture site. Some types of fracture are caused by diseased bone and, in these cases, the cause needs to be identified before the appropriate treatment is known.

In some of these cases it may be counterproductive to immobilise the bone. In most cases painkillers are of benefit. Consult the vet as soon as you suspect a fracture has occurred.

HYPERTHERMIA

Hyperthermia (overheating) can rapidly kill Bearded Dragons. Often they are just found dead. If alive, they will feel hot to the touch with their mouth gaping, or they may be comatose. This can happen on a hot day when the Bearded Dragon has no access to shade.

Temperatures can also quickly reach lethal levels in glass or plastic vivaria exposed to direct sunlight, or even through a glass window. Any temperature above 38 degree C (100.4 F) may lead to hyperthermia (juveniles are more susceptible).

Immediately remove the Bearded Dragon from the heat into a cool area. Immerse the lizard in cool, not cold, water, making sure that it does not drown by supporting its head. There may be irreversible damage done to internal organs, especially the brain.

Contact your vet immediately. Medical treatment, which needs to be started as soon as possible, may include intra-osseous fluids to support the circulation, oxygen for improved breathing and drugs to try to prevent swelling of the brain.

If the Dragon recovers, it may be unable to thermo-regulate due to damage to that part of the brain called the thermo-regulatory centre. This means that it will not seek shade, as normal Bearded Dragons would when their bodies start to overheat. It would be predisposed to future episodes.

With good care and management, your Bearded Dragon should live a healthy life, suffering few health problems.